Mr Kazarian
Alien Librarian

by Steve Foxe
illustrated by Gary Boller

THE ASTEROID EXCURSION

2

I never *planned* to reveal my mission to my Earthling students. But it's often happy accidents that lead to the greatest discoveries!

Now that my brilliant young students know who – and what – I am, I've been helping them explore the universe around them.

And while they learn about the universe, I learn about *them!* Fascinating creatures.

Hurry up, Mr K!

(TJ is still learning patience, it seems.)

There's so much to explore beyond planet Earth. Our only challenge is making it back to school before Mrs Tsao notices we're gone!

Yes, Shea?

Mr Snow, you're telling me the Greek soldiers hid inside this giant, fake horse? And the other guys fell for it?

TROJAN HORSE

Well, Shea —

Oh!

Walden! Are you all right?

Can't you guys hear that noise? It's *so* strange!

Huh? I can't hear anything.

Back to your seats, students.

Walden, your hearing aid might be playing up.

Is it painful?

No, but it's distracting.

Dani, since you're a school safety officer, why don't you escort Walden to the nurse's office?

5

DIINNNGGG!

I hope Walden's hearing aid is fixed. I thought they'd be back before class ended.

I'm sure he's fine! He probably just picked up the local radio station again.

Meaaaowwr!

Quark! What are you doing here? If Mrs Tsao sees you, she'll have a sneezing fit.

I don't speak cat, but I think that's the sign for "follow me".

Quark is pointing towards the library!

I have to say, my mums are proud that I'm spending so much time surrounded by books.

How many have you actually read?

Hey, our "library" adventures are just as educational as books!

TJ, quiet! What if someone hears?

Hears what?

Remember, Quark fixed it so we say "librarian" when we really mean... "you know what".

Secret's safe with us!

6

Our young friend Walden picked up an unusual signal on his device.

I thought my hearing aid was on the blink...

...but it turns out it was a message -- from *space!*

We came straight here so we could talk about the alien signal without using code words!

Did the signal come from another Pflittlehornian?

Oh dorplux, no. But we'll soon know who *did* send it.

This is an antique mento-visualiser I picked up from an orbital jumble sale. If it still works, we should be able to turn the signal Walden received into a hologram.

I call dibs on the mega-video-geyser next! I have loads of ideas that the world needs to see in 4D!

Visualiser. And it's not a toy, TJ. It's a complex scientific instrument.

Ah, success! It looks like...

The asteroid belt!

That's right, Shea! Excellent observation. Those rocky objects are called asteroids. They orbit your sun. Some are quite small. Others are hundreds of kilometres across!

Dani and I have been working on a video-game coding project for house points.

It's all about *blasting* asteroids!

Did you know that asteroids are left over from the beginning of this universe, 4.6 billion years ago? We only get new asteroids when two collide and pieces break off. But that's rare.

There are three types of aster -- oh, look! The mento-visualizer is zooming in to the exact source of Walden's mystery signal!

11

I do so admire your bravery and drive...

...but I simply must put my tentacle down.

This asteroid excursion is too dangerous.

However, I *will* send a distress signal to Quark's collar should I need help.

If that happens, you can use my blorgcorder to contact the Pflittlehornian council. They'll know what to do.

Aww man, I really thought that learning angle was going to convince him.

Yeah, guess we don't get a "field trip" today after all.

You boys give up fast, eh?

Seriously.

Mr K said Quark's collar could receive his signal, right?

Which means we can probably use it to track Mr K too!

We just have to wait for him to leave...

...and let ourselves back in.

Since when are you two the rule-breakers?

That's my gig!

We're not breaking any rules. Even if we can't fly off with him, maybe we can at least cheer him on from here!

And those adorable colony aliens. Plus, maybe we really *will* learn something about asteroids that we can use in our game!

13

Almost...got it!

Look at Mr K go! He's got to be violating intergalactic speed laws.

It looks like he's heading for Mars.

Is that where the asteroid belt is?

Correct, Earthling! The asteroid belt in your solar system can be found between Mars and Jupiter.

Whoa, it's a Kazarian cartoon!

Mr K must have programmed his console's helper to look like himself. I want a cartoon me too!

The real version of you is goofy enough, TJ.

I wonder what else this mini Mr K can tell us, though.

How many asteroids are in the asteroid belt?

Far too many for you humans to count. There are millions of asteroids in the asteroid belt.

However, the four *largest* asteroids in the asteroid belt account for more than *half* of the asteroid belt's entire mass.

Cartoon Kazarian is very educational, but we're trying to snoop on the real Mr K!

Why did you not say so? I'll set the back-up shuttle to autopilot, following the path set by my creator.

Back-up shuttle?

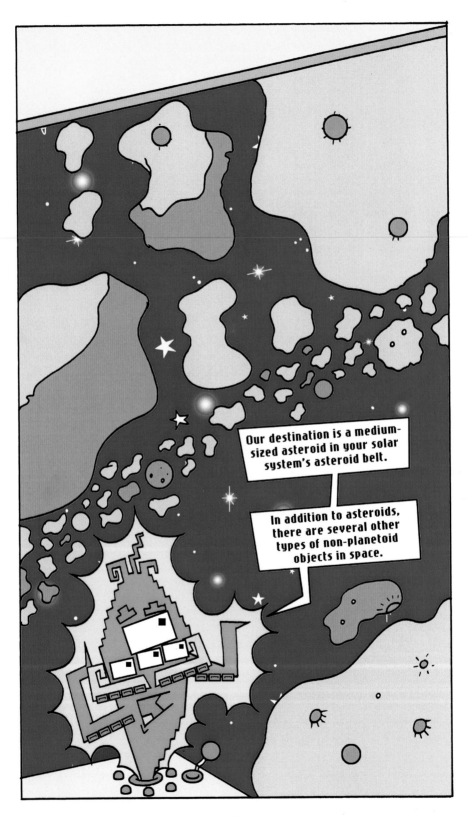

...for take-off!
I...said... MEDIUM!
You will learn some additional facts during transit!
It sounds like we don't have a choice!
Wow. Cats really can sleep through anything.

20

Meteoroids can form when asteroids and comets collide with other objects. Or they can break off on their own.

Many millions of meteors enter Earth's atmosphere every day. Most of them are tiny. Almost all of them burn up on entry.

Sometimes many meteors enter the same area in a short period of time. Humans call this a *meteor shower*.

Most meteorites are so small that no one ever notices them. Others are large enough to be preserved in your museums.

And some meteorites are so large that they leave massive impact craters. The largest meteorite crater ever discovered was in South Africa. It has a diameter of nearly *300 kilometres*!

That's a pretty big crater. Should we -- *gulp* -- be afraid of meteorites like that crashing onto *us*?

Weren't you listening, short human? As I clearly explained, most meteorites are quite small.

The last time an object from space caused an extinction-level event on Earth was more than 66 million years ago.

I don't think Mr Kazarian's hologram knows how to talk to kids as well as real Mr K does...

At any rate, we have reached our destination. My program will end once the ship comes to a stop.

25

There's breathable air in here! We can turn off our suits.

Ahh, fresh, alien air.

Guys! I could do with that help! Any day now!

Uhhh...?

Dani! It's a picture of *you*! You're like their Mona Lisa!

Do you have any alien relatives, Dani?

Mr Kazarian!

He's been attacked!

What are you four doing here? And Quark too! I thought I said this trip was too dangerous!

It's a good thing we didn't listen! You look like you got caught in a meteor shower.

You're not far off, TJ. When I approached the asteroid colony, some debris left over from the collision hit my ship!

Thankfully, the Arrok are a peaceful, kind species. They've been taking good care of me, despite having their own troubles.

But how has that happened already? We left *straight* after you did.

Ah, but the back-up shuttle is slower than my primary transportation. It took you a blimwad or two longer than me to get here.

How did you pass the time on the trip? I know the back-up shuttle isn't exactly the height of comfort.

We had Cartoon Kazarian to keep us company!

He taught us the difference between comets, meteoroids, meteors and meteorites.

Cartoon Kazarian...ah, you mean the A.I. I programmed! Oh how wonderful!

I'm glad Kaz 2.0 was able to assist!

Maybe you can assist *him* on his people skills.

TJ's not wrong. Kaz 2.0 ditched us as soon as we landed!

And now these aliens think I'm their *hero*!

Real Mr Kazarian is definitely better than hologram Mr Kazarian...

Ah, that's very kind of you to say, Walden! But Kaz 2.0 will be helpful in finding the other half of the Arrok colony asteroid.

We must reunite their community!

The first human to ever identify an asteroid was Giuseppe Piazzi, an astronomer from the area you call Italy. This was in the year 1801, by your calendar.

Two hundred years *before* Piazzi lived, Tycho Brahe from Denmark was looking up at the sky. He greatly advanced the standard for astronomical measurements.

Brahe's studies made charting objects in space much more precise. And he was one of the last Earth astronomers to work *without* a telescope.

He also had a brass nose, which I believe is rare among humans!

One of Brahe's students was Johannes Kepler, who came from Germany. He played a big role in your planet's scientific revolution in the 1600s.

KEPLER

He was inspired to study astronomy as a child, after he saw a large comet pass overhead.

Kepler lived around the same time as the legendary Earth scientist Galileo Galilei.

The two often disagreed. But their research led to amazing breakthroughs for your species.

Kepler's grandest achievements were his laws of planetary motion. He discovered that all the large objects in the solar system rotate around the sun in a sort of oval pattern.

All of *that* knowledge helped Giuseppe Piazzi discover the first asteroid, named Ceres. It is the largest object in the asteroid belt.

Ceres is nearly 950 kilometres in diameter. It makes up a third of the mass of the *entire* asteroid belt!

Ceres is *so* large that Earth scientists have classified it as a dwarf planet, like Pluto.

The term *asteroid* means "star-shaped" in Greek. It was made popular in 1802 by the British astronomer William Herschel.

Herschel discovered many things -- including Uranus, infrared radiation and some of the most famous moons in your solar system!

HERSCHEL

The Herschel Space Observatory satellite was named after him.

It was the largest infrared telescope ever launched by planet Earth. It operated from 2009 until 2013.

37

TJ! Watch your bubble gum. We have guests.

POP!

I told you before, TJ -- most of the galaxy considers your chewing gum to be horrible torture!

We are nearly at our destination. Kaz 2.0 is doing a splendid job of navigating the asteroid belt.

Good job programming me, real-me.

Why, thank you, Holo-Me.

41

Mr K, what's a carbon asteroid?

Ah, I got ahead of myself for a womplegorg.

There are three main types of asteroids: carbon asteroids, stony asteroids and metallic asteroids. They are also called C-type, S-type and M-type asteroids.

More than 75 per cent of asteroids are carbon asteroids.

They're dark in colour and made up of rocks rich in the element carbon.

Stony asteroids are made up of rocks, occasionally with some metal.

Metallic asteroids, on the other hand, are mostly metal with some stone mixed in. The most common metals in these asteroids are iron and nickel.

CLANK

Not all asteroids are found in the asteroid belt. Asteroids that share orbits with planets or moons, but don't collide with them, are called Trojan asteroids. This is because they "hide" behind the objects they follow.

Kind of like the Trojan Horse story we learnt today!

Precisely! But Trojan asteroids hide *behind* objects, not *in* them!

Most Trojan asteroids orbit near Jupiter. There may be as many Trojan asteroids in the solar system as there are asteroids in the asteroid belt!

Learning time is over! We're approaching our destination.

Maybe you were right... I should fine-tune Kaz 2.0's attitude programs...

44

We should have this ship repaired by the time your -- what did you call him, librarian? -- is back!

I know the hologram Mr K told us not to worry about giant asteroids hitting Earth...

...but I'm worried anyway!

You mean meteorites! But don't work yourself up, Dani.

There's almost no chance of that happening.

Hey, what did you find, buddy?

Meoow!

KRACK

Oh no -- we're being bombarded with METEORITES *right now!*

Wait, what about Wils?

He's talking to me through my hearing aid.

He must be sending a signal from inside Mr K's ship!

Great hero's friend! If you can hear me, please turn on the colony's extra defence shields.

Without them, there won't *be* a colony for our friends to return to!

He says we need to turn on the shields. What are we going to do?

You heard him. We have to get those shields up!

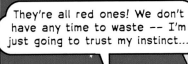

48

49

What will the Arrok do now, Mr K? They can't stay on this broken asteroid, can they?

Now that Colony-426 is reunited, the Arrok can repair any damages. Then they can move on to their next destination.

I've decided to give them Kaz 2.0, to help them assess new locations and better predict incoming space debris!

Aww, I'll kind of miss you, Kaz 2.0.

I will not miss you, Earthling, for I am a machine program with no feelings.

Goodbye!

Well...never mind then.

Hmph.

Your shuttle is repaired, Mr Kazarian. We've attached a cable to your back-up craft, so you can tow it back to Earth.

Thank you again for all of your help, and for bringing us the great hero!

Bye Wils! Thanks for all the confidence! Good luck!

I really must thank you kids for following me despite my request that you stay on Earth. Without your help and Kaz 2.0, the Arrok might still be stranded.

Mrowrrrrr!

Yes Quark, you too.

And I'm so thrilled you were able to learn about asteroids, meteoroids, comets and other space facts in the midst of all the action.

After all, asteroids have been travelling through space for more than 4.6 *billion* years.

Just think of the history they hold within them!

And there are countless asteroids and meteors and other space rocks zooming past Earth every single day -- more than we could ever count!

Kinda...scary if you think about it.

That's a lot of rocks.

Don't fear, TJ. Scientists on your planet track asteroids that may approach Earth's atmosphere. They've even considered plans to blow up asteroids in the atmosphere before they could reach the planet.

That...is...so...COOL!

Well, I hope our little trip hasn't made you late for your next lesson.

No worries, Mr K. It was worth it just for that amazing "tennis" game!

I've found my new favourite sport!

There you four are. It's time for science class! Where have you been? And what happened to you, Mr Kazarian?!

He got hit by falling...

Books!

Yeah, Shea and I needed a book from the top shelf.

We accidentally knocked a few over.

Then Dani saved the day, like a boss! And we got the colony -- er, Mr K -- all patched up.

Well. Sounds like Mr Kazarian was lucky to have you kids around. But you really must get a pass next time you spend your study time in the library.

Later...

Mr Kazarian, I'm glad you weren't injured too badly. You really bring the adventures in your books to life, judging by the state of these students!

Research log number 14,367:

My studies here on Earth have offered no shortage of excitement. I'm still sore from this latest excursion!

Shea, TJ, Dani and Walden followed their instincts and arrived just in time to help those in need.

I considered the entire expedition too dangerous, but these brave humans didn't give up. They even found moments to delight in the action.

More importantly, they acted without hesitation, rising to the occasion when there was no time to waste.

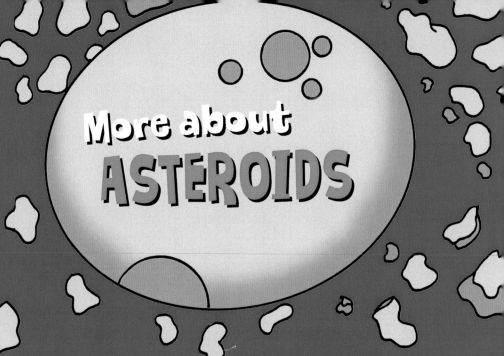

More about ASTEROIDS

- Asteroids are also known as planetoids or minor planets. They are made of rock and metal, and they orbit the sun.

- Unlike the planets in our solar system, many asteroids are lumpy and oddly shaped because they don't have their own gravity rounding them out.

- Asteroids are similar to comets, but they lack the bright outline and tail, or coma, that defines comets.

- Asteroids come in a wide range of sizes, from just 10 metres (33 feet) across to hundreds of kilometres. Objects under 10 metres in diameter are usually considered meteoroids.

- Most of the asteroids in our solar system reside in the asteroid belt between Mars and Jupiter. There are millions of asteroids within the asteroid belt.

- The first asteroid ever discovered was Ceres, which orbits within the asteroid belt. Italian astronomer Giuseppe Piazzi first spotted it in 1801.

- Ceres is now considered a dwarf planet because of its large size. The other dwarf planets in our solar system are Pluto, Eris, Makemake and Haumea.

- Asteroids regularly come close to or even hit Earth, but most burn up when they enter our atmosphere. Most scientists believe that a large asteroid collision 66 million years ago led to the extinction of the dinosaurs.

- Asteroids also contain organic compounds. Some scientists think asteroids hitting Earth billions of years ago helped introduce the elements needed for life to begin on the planet.

- Meteoroids are smaller objects that formed when our universe began. They are usually less than 10 metres in diameter.

- Meteoroids that enter Earth's atmosphere and burn up are called meteors. Meteors are sometimes called "shooting stars", and several of them entering the atmosphere in a short amount of time is called a meteor shower or storm.

- Meteoroids that make it to the surface of Earth without burning up are called meteorites.

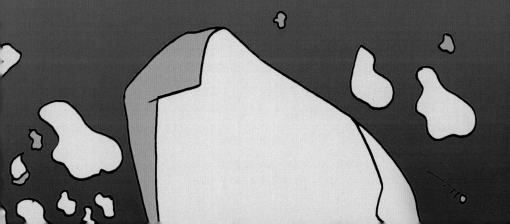

Glossary

asteroid chunk of rock and metal left over from the solar system's formation; asteroids orbit the sun but are too small to be considered planets

carbon asteroid asteroid that is dark in colour and made up of rocks rich in the element carbon

coma heated gas that trails behind a comet

comet ball of ice, rock and dust that clumped together when the universe was formed and now orbits the sun

diameter distance measured straight through an object's centre

dwarf planet round object that orbits the sun but isn't large enough to qualify as a planet

impact crater bowl-shaped landform created by a meteorite crashing into a planet

metallic asteroid asteroid that is mainly metal with some stone mixed in; the most common metals in these asteroids are iron and nickel

meteor meteoroid that gets pulled into Earth's atmosphere by the planet's gravity

meteorite meteor that reaches Earth's surface without burning up

meteoroid small piece of rock or metal that has broken off a comet or asteroid

prototype first version of an invention that tests an idea to see if it will work

stony asteroid asteroid made up of rocks, occasionally with some metal

Trojan asteroid asteroid that orbits with planets or moons, but doesn't collide with them

Deep thoughts
with Mr Kazarian

- It can be difficult to remember the difference between meteors, meteorites and meteoroids. If you had to teach a friend or classmate about these objects, how would you explain the differences?

- The Arrok move from asteroid to asteroid, setting up new homes as they go. Have you ever moved home? What was it like? If you could live somewhere else in the world, where would you move and why?

- Mr Kazarian and the kids have to use a translator to understand the Arrok. Have you ever met someone who speaks a different language? How did you communicate with them?

Find out more

Can You Survive an Asteroid Strike? (You Choose: Doomsday), Matt Doeden (Raintree, 2018)

Exploring Meteor Showers (Discover the Night Sky), Brigid Gallagher (Raintree, 2018)

Planet Hunting: Racking Up Data and Looking for Life (Future Space), Andrew Langley (Raintree, 2020)

Steve →

Steve Foxe is the author of more than 40 children's books and comics for characters including Pokémon, Transformers, Adventure Time, Steven Universe, DC Super Friends and Grumpy Cat. He lives in New York, USA, where he and his dog dodge falling meteorites.

Gary →

Gary Boller is an illustrator and animator based in London. He has written and illustrated many children's books and comics, including strips for *The Beano*, *The Dandy* and *The Times*. He also works in advertising and entertainment, including the Bafta-winning animated series, *The Amazing Adrenalini Brothers*. Gary is never very far away from a cat and is unwittingly helping cats take control of this planet.

Raintree is an imprint of Capstone Global Library Limited, a company
incorporated in England and Wales having its registered office at 264
Banbury Road, Oxford, OX2 7DY – Registered company number: 6695582

www.raintree.co.uk
myorders@raintree.co.uk

Edited by Kristen Mohn
Designed by Ted Williams
Original illustrations © Capstone Global Library Limited 2021
Production by Tori Abraham
Originated by Capstone Global Library Ltd

978 1 3982 0359 4

British Library Cataloguing in Publication Data
A full catalogue record for this book is available from the British Library.

Printed and bound in the United Kingdom